Feeling All My Fear

Kim T. S.

This book belongs to:

It's okay to feel scared!
It's how your body warns you of danger and keeps you safe. Understanding and facing it can help you overcome your fear. Find a grown-up you trust to help you through it... someone who helps you feel safe.

It can be hard to talk about your feelings, but there are other ways to do it. You can write it down, draw it, show pictures, or act it out! Keep asking for help until you feel better.

You are not alone.

♡ Kim

Published by Kim T. S. - Doña Hemady St., Quezon City, Philippines
www.kimtsbooks.com

For anyone who has ever felt scared and alone... remember there is always someone who cares.

There are times Ellie shows
all the things that she feels.

There are times she pretends
what she feels isn't real.

Let it go...

It's okay to feel feelings,
then let them all go.
We all feel those feelings...
you're strong, don't you know?

It’s okay
even if
you feel scared
of the dark.

It’s okay for you
to feel scared of a shark!

It's okay to feel scared
of things that aren't scary...
like a lamp, or a cow,
or a man who is hairy!

Others might think
what you're scared of is weird.
They might think it's something
that shouldn't be feared.

What's not scary for you
may be scary for me.
We're all different---
that's how it should be!

anger
worry
happiness
envy
sadness
grief
fear

ALL FEELINGS ARE Okay!

Emotions hold meaning;
feeling scared isn't bad.
There are no bad feelings,
though some drive you mad!

Fear keeps you alert
and safe from all harm.
When danger is near,
it sounds the alarm!

danger!

Why are you scared?
What is it you fear?
Tell a grown-up you trust
who will listen and hear.

You can work together
to find a good way
for you to feel safe;
you'll soon be okay.

And if you are safe, but still you feel scared,
remember it helps if you are prepared.

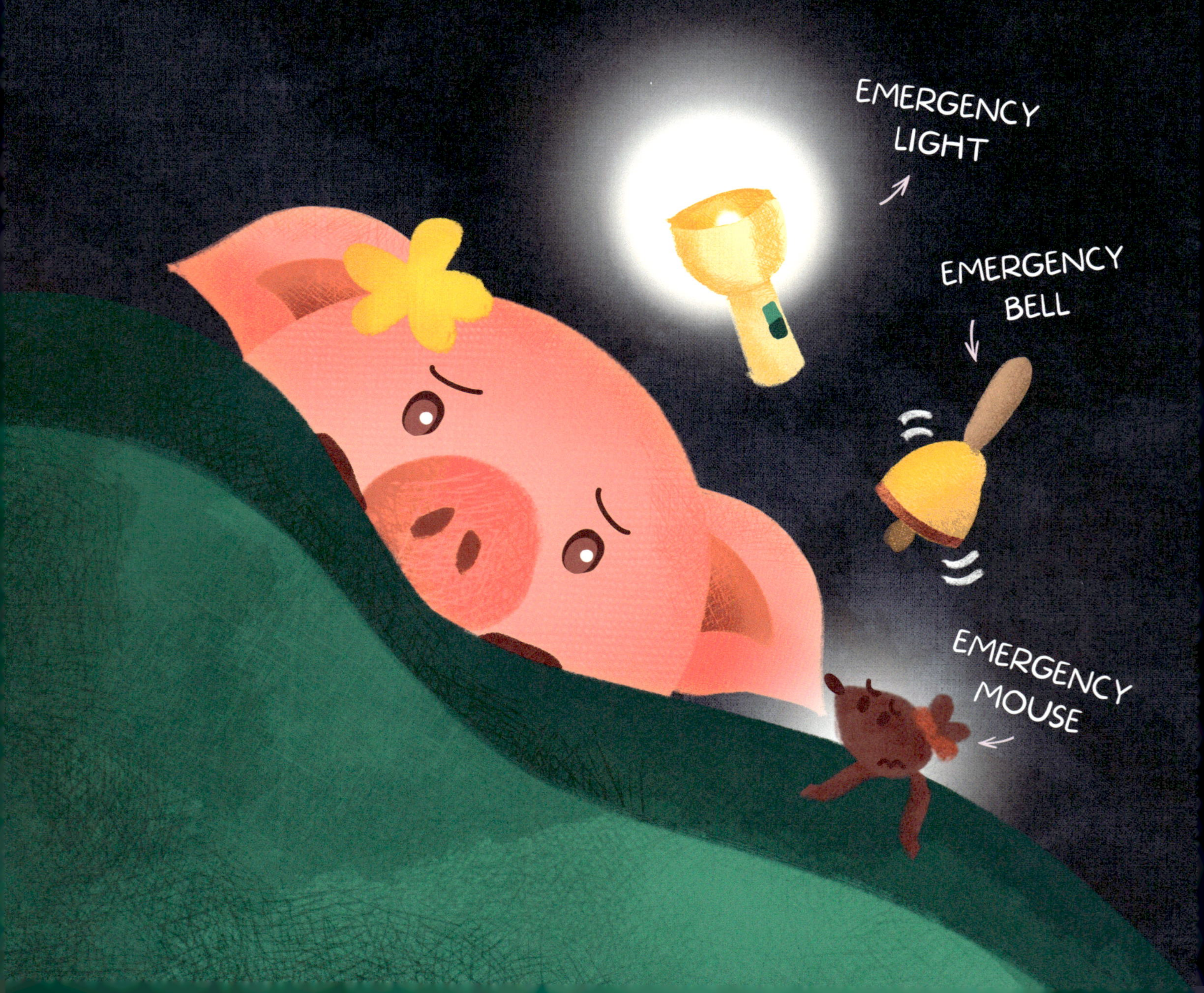

Perhaps there's a way for you to be brave;
to face that big fear and ride that big wave!

Let's try to pretend
you have magic glasses
that let you see fear
as a feeling that passes.

They show you quite well
what others can see...

and help you show why
you're as scared as can be!

If it's hard for you to imagine why others aren't scared, try to ask them. Explain how you feel so they'll understand you.

If you can see from another perspective,
you can become an emotions detective.

How can I feel the way others are feeling? It seems so much better than hiding and reeling.

Maybe I'll think of something that's funny;
maybe the dark can become
bright and sunny.

I know it's not easy, but I know I can do it.
To feel more than one feeling
is all there is to it!

Look for the love
and comfort around you;

you can find peace,
with some help, if you try to.

Those beasts aren't here,
so don't let them steal
the comfort you feel...
please let your heart heal.

But if you still find yourself
nervous and frightened,
check if you're safe
so the dark can be brightened.

Your mind's like a muscle;
make it stronger each day.
There's power inside you
to chase fear away!

Even when scared,
you can feel brave and strong;
In time you will find
it's been there all along.

Your feedback inspires us to keep writing!

If our books have helped you in any way, please let us know through a message or review!

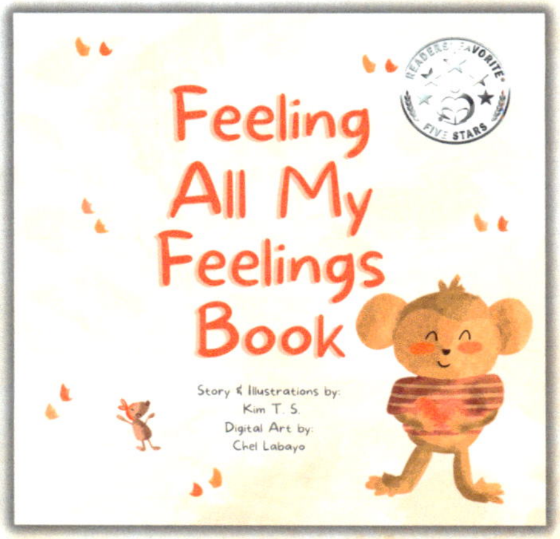

Review us on amazon

Want freebies?

Get FREE emotional regulation activity sheets when you sign up to our mailing list. Use your smartphone camera to scan the code below, then tap the link.
Or visit our website!

SCAN ME

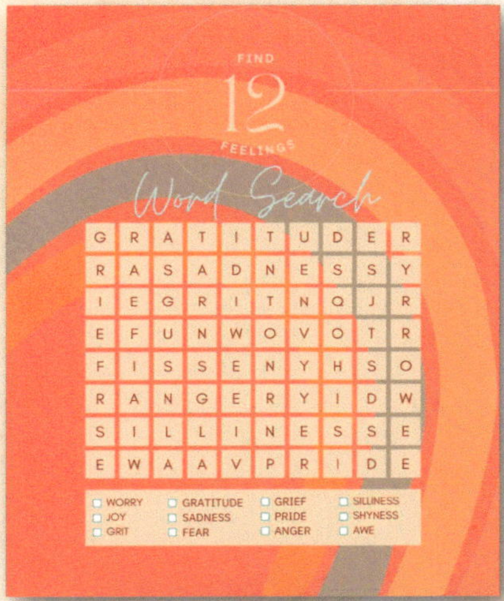

@kimt.s.books - @kimtsbooks
kimtsbooks@gmail.com

www.kimtsbooks.com

What will you do the next time you feel scared?

Draw your own scene and email it to kimtsbooks@gmail.com.

Or post it on social media and tag us @kimtsbooks!

www.kimtsbooks.com

Made in United States
Troutdale, OR
03/14/2025

29759404R00024